Lovers *in the* Free Fall

Also by the author

The Red Thread
Boat of the Dream
Beyond Words
Body India
Family Salt
Burning Through

LOVERS *in the*
FREE FALL

Elizabeth Gordon McKim

Poems
Stories
Songs

Leapfrog Press
Fredonia, New York

Published in 2020 in the United States by
Leapfrog Press LLC
PO Box 505
Fredonia, NY 14063
www.leapfrogpress.com

Printed in the United States of America

Distributed in the United States by
Consortium Book Sales and Distribution
St. Paul, Minnesota 55114
www.cbsd.com

Cover Image: "Angurria for Beyond Walls Street Art Festival 2017 in Lynn, MA"

Author photo by Wes Chester

First Edition

Library of Congress Cataloging-in-Publication Data

Names: McKim, Elizabeth, author.
Title: Lovers in the free fall : poems / Elizabeth Gordon McKim.
Description: First Edition. | Fredonia, New York: Leapfrog Press, 2020. |
  Summary: "A rich and diverse array of poems, stories, and songs, fully
  realized and embodied, both local and far flung, meant to be heard,
  enjoyed and carried into the reader's own life and times. In her sixth
  collection of poetry, "the Jazz Poet of Lynn" offers the reader a wide
  range of forms and shapes: sestinas, haikus, free verse, blues and
  ballads, myths and memory. They carry the narrative thread through the
  rhythm and pulse of beginnings, change, and continuance. Both local and
  far-flung, these poems are meant to be heard, enjoyed, and carried into
  the reader's own life"-- Provided by publisher.
Identifiers: LCCN 2020006002 | ISBN 9781948585118 (trade paperback)
Subjects: LCGFT: Poetry.
Classification: LCC PS3563.A3168 L68 2020 | DDC 811/.54--dc23
LC record available at https://lccn.loc.gov/2020006002

Lovers *in the* Free Fall

DEDICATION

Thanks and again thanks
For the whole lovely kit n' caboodle
Our particular and specific lives offer up
Can't say it was or wasn't a blast/
Or a bust or an easy treaty or a pocketbook of lies
Or a sack of sighs or a crazy maze
But we are here and I am infinitely
Amazed to know you/ to breathe beside
You and to walk among you
So again gracias, merci, amen
And yeah thanks
All ways along this fragile bridge,
This great trajectory, this tiny history
This long-lost promontory, not to be forgotten
And never the whole story and yes thanks
From the faraway ridge, and over and out
Into the air
No despair/ no despair/ no despair

Lovers/ Lovers/ Lovers in the free-fall now
Lovers in the free fall/ Lovers in the free fall

Lovers in the free fall now

CONTENTS

Places/Spaces

Motion/Commotion

CLOSING/OPENING

OPENING/CLOSING

DREAM 2004: 13 WILLOW ST, LYNN MA

I am sleeping it is september round and golden in my new home an old shoe
Factory renovated . . . in the middle of a delicious afternoon nap stolen decisive all
Day I have felt the clouds chimneys seagulls soldiers a woman stepping out in
A red hat men and women dying in baghdad the smell of it 14,000 detainees at
Prisons around the world . . . how do you spread this democracy like rancid
Mayo . . . everyone is getting sick dragging the dead across an abandoned minefield
That once was a dance floor now a noxious pit. . . .

I am sleeping without a quilt on the purple couch bought from carlos and david
On the first floor I am sleeping the windows are wide open the sounds
Of the streets filter into my dreams I can hear the bell of the commuter train
I can see the gulu gulu café named after a café in prague an african man in a pin-
Striped suit walks around the corner talking into his cell phone the leaves of the tree
Tremble and glint into the late afternoon sounds of cars like waves as in maine
I see the rock like a tablet a fish engraved on it floated over from ireland
Eons ago it was carved by one of the early saints a sign of the fish. . . .

I'm dreaming and suddenly there is a musical sound someone sitting by my side
Waiting for me . . . someone has let him in he comes to say goodbye or hello
Not quite sure what is happening he kisses me lightly a few times on my lips
My first lover not my first boyfriend my first lover . . . we smile surrounding
Each other I smile through my sleep I am so happy you have come
An aria. . . .

THE OPENING AND CLOSING

Of petals sleek as the backs of fish
their gills opening into the black
spreading out into a darker ink
closing down the wild field of day
the sureness the depth of the woman
the man in the mirror behind her the darkness
behind him the way their eyes open the light the world presses
inside the laundry outside
filling with wind creasing back
into a pocket the morning sun stretches
into afternoon marking sun
down the whole stain of day the birds heel
out into the wound the dark closes
as I open to my love as he closes we become
the secret petals pulse the house
the prisoner the presence the furthest exit
now he opens as I close I remember scenes
I didn't expect the young Vietnamese whose mouth
burns mine closed the years open Mesopotamia
my eyes leap into my daughter's open face in fright in friendliness
as I close over the final fact now open
and staring a fish closed and hooked
slapping its bloody weight
across the open deck

WATCH

In the cusp
of loving
I skim lonely
in precise places
near your home
I watch you
from up-
side/ the head
from water-
bed, from book
of the dead
from gibbous
to full/ moon
from cow
jump over
the salty spoon
from telephone call
from duluth
from empty booth
from broken tooth
from 2 roads
on the earth
both taken
from 2 tongues
shaken/ from bring home the beacon/ from easter
from ramadan/ from pesach/ from birth
from the mirror/ from mirth
from thunder/ from/ the bridge
from the air
from water/ from fire
from the muck n' mire
from what we share
from our local/ quicksilver/ lair
from when you look at me
from when I look at you

from the door
from when we go/ home
we go home together
two/ together
gather ro/ses ro/ses
washed in the blood of the ordinary life

LETTER

I want to send you a letter
You have never received
I want to send it
In the morning
At first light
But if I have to
I will send it at noon
Or I will send it
If need be
At dusk
Or even if I must
I will send it at midnight
Or in the lost hours of the wolf
When you cannot sleep

I want to know the sound of your steps
In the city where you survive
I want to know how you breathe

in the space
between

one leaf
its jagged edge

one stone
scarred

one face
at the broken
window

I want to know your evenings
How they spread out before you
And your mornings the sound of your starlings
I want to know your ragged stars

LAY/ABOUT

As if searching weren't enough she relinquished this activity to something sharper and often, deeper. Yes friends she gave up searching, she couldn't do it any longer, and she was hard pressed to know why, even when she couldn't find something, like scissors or the here/after, like warrants or lay/about summons, or the shy buds of april magnolias in boston along common/wealth avenue, or those first indications of adolescence in a granddaughter only four and a half, one loving wands and frothy tutus, so much like herself at that age, yes friends, every afternoon these winter days, she lay down and gave up searching for anything, and dreams wandered by paying their respects, offering condolences, appearing for no realizable reason, just to say hi, just to say they'd come by to see how she was doing, or not doing, laying about as she was.

DESTINATIONS/TRANS/MIGRATIONS

I FORGOT TO TELL YOU SOMETHING
TERRIBLE AND BEAUTIFUL

Watering this small plant
   covered with road dust, half dead in tire tracks
      and gasoline fumes, I forgot to tell you about
         what is here and else where

How as a child driving in the car at night
   I would lean into the enormity of my father
      and feel suddenly safe, fear falling off me
         like water, I would remember the overgrown

Thicket behind our house near where my ma hung out the laundry
   and where sometimes I would go to feel something
      anything, in the scattering sky, wondering
         why I was forever being born

How way past older now
   rebounding from the usual flinty sparks and remarks
      I wished for before, emerging in the unseasonable
         weather, looping and doubling across the arbitrary

Borders, I come upon these blazing discs of memory:
   arcs flung up against the baffling sky

AMONG

All these others, on the way home, she listened
To remarks among swirled conch shells
On city windows calling, caterwauling
Old time remedies/ leading bass violins/ leased
Barbershop poles/ subterraneous particles

Among barn owl's scarred remains

Speech of hand/ shake/ eye / blink / ghosts
Of goodbye/ problematic/ equations/ faraway/ tsunami
Devastated countries/ defunct parts /burnt
Out architecture/ molded memories / hemp
Woven belligerently into battle trenches
Aromas and scents/ lingering inside winter
Coats/ moldy/ match books/ newly ground/ whole
Bean coffee/ damp heat of sex, of skin, of root
Of rutabaga, of casual encounter, sudden
And serious, she loved the clean causal
Squeak of things she lived among:

Voluptuous sap nighttime repair
Tracks of wild and skittish creatures
Stunning cries of former times
Old ways, now/ turning
Here and there
She listens
Among

MIGRATION

Remember I did not choose to be who I am
Remember the deep ocean where I was born
How I moved on the soft sands
There were days even then I did not know who I was
My body was washed with the stain of the singing
It bled in the darkness
There were creatures even then
Even in the darkness, their shapeless heat
Nudging my heart. I gave them my milk, all that I had.
We grew drowsy and plump.
We lay on our backs
Exchanging stories of earth and air.
We grew strong.
We stopped going home we dispersed we returned
Stammering at first we became a band we swarmed
Over beds and shelves, borders and promontories,
We were stopped at the frontier, we answered no
To all questions we were asked to produce
Evidence
We had none.
Our bodies could not lie. We took to hiding out.
Some of us tried to find our old names our former homes.
All was destroyed.
It was painful.
I fell behind. My friends nursed me to health.
They held me at night when I was simply afraid
And soaked in my fear.
We were not saved, even in the end,
Our mouths swollen and overwhelmed with songs

SAY HELLO

Out on the high
Way hitching
To nirvana
Ginger and curry
Pasted on my open
Palms

I wake up
In San Diego
The desert rolls up
To the street curb
In a gold limo
You step out like a star
Meanwhile the parakeets
Are parked in the palm trees
In front of Von's

They wave
A gold-blue salute
Then disappear
Into the flat blank
California sky
PS I am here on the left
Coast and you back east
Up to the hilt
In snow
Say hello

SWISS COWS

Visiting Swiss cows
Their bell sounds tumble down hills
Sweeten the valleys

I greet my cow friends
Their bodies turn into mountains
Transcending ass end

Their soul pooling eyes
Their long articulate spines
Cow manure smell

A huge lime green
Grasshopper hops on my shoe
I head home to lunch

HAVING COME TO PARIS

Having come this far
You startled me, fear,
And I knew I could go nowhere
You are not
As simple as that
We exist together
Like wild mushrooms
At the side of the driveway in maine
Or in the *recoin de l'église*
In the corner of the church
Or at the back of the bus
Or crouched on the paris sidewalk with yr little dog
Holding yr paper cup
Making small vowel sounds with yr mouth
You weren't much to look at, fear,
But I loved you on sight
And wanted to take you home
If I could only find home
I found you with your limp
With your feet that could not move as they used to
I found you home from the useless wars
I found you taking photos in front of the literary café
Do you remember that jubilant afternoon when I met you, fear,
Walking down the street toward me
The same street my children and grandchildren walk
I spotted you
With no makeup or put down or mask
Only a simple fear on a simple day
Waiting for something to happen
So the storm might break
Or at least come on full blast
And we could all go home
And munch on fresh made cookies
And drink something warm
Fear give me your hand

I'm asking you flat out and clear
Listen to me
Across the street *la pharmacie*
Blinks a green neon cross
And people are putting up umbrellas
And installing their rain hats
Inside the café simone de beauvoir writes all night and day
While outside 2 small sparrows hop
On the yellow and green wicker chairs
While the three losers in my novel house of sand and fog
Want only a simple expression of passion
To provide a homecoming
Or a red dot in the corner of the painting
Is that too much to ask
I ask you, fear?

LA LUNE ET LE TROTTOIR –
THE MOON AND THE SIDE WALK

Mais qu'est-ce qu'il y a? / Hey what's goin' on?

La lune est sur le trottoir / The moon is on the sidewalk

Et le trottoir brille / And the sidewalk is shining

Mais écoutes cheri / But listen sweetheart

La lune ne coute rien / The moon costs nothing

Et le trottoir? / And the sidewalk?

Tout tout tout tout / All all all

Ce que tu es / All that you are

Ça alors! Laisses-la tranquille / Hey! Give me a break

Je t'en pris / I'm beggin' ya

Regardes cherie / Hey look sweetie

Le trottoir se respire maintenant / The sidewalk is breathing into itself

Secret! Passionant! / Secret! Passionate!

Et la lune? / And the moon?

La lune est dure et inflexible. /

The moon is tough. The moon will not give in.

ALARM

Outside my window
Monarch butterflies streak by
And I hear mother

Can't tell what she wants
But I know something's wrong
From her high-pitched cry

OUR MA

born under the skirts of victoria
(whatever that means)
she says take the toys
away from the boys
six wars
a man's world
her father's darling child
but she could never sit in his chair
dare to presume
so she sighed the large sighs
my mother and her mother
and her mother before her
happiest time was when she was
hub of her family's universe
her husband surrounding her
and then he went and took off
his earthy clothes
that old slipaway
and then
she bled her life away
among the wobbly dolls
in the nursing home corridor
ethel wails
like an ancient crow
albert albert take a right take a right
oh no oh no
genevieve counts backwards/ steals my mama's bed
we come and go
bring things beside the point
of death which does its draining
they want to hook her up
and give her tests
and take her to a hospital
we hold firm
my sisters either side of me

three of us
we hold our course
succinct succinct
the caulking voice of death
i dream a bee and hummingbird
circle round the door and dwelling place
what's happening to me
am i dying

MOTHER'S LAMENT

Persephone. Come home.
We search for you everywhere.
We need you home. Now.

Go to Sambisa
Forest. Find the girls. Bring them
Home. Bring our girls home.

So much disappears
Around daughters. Seasons. Salt.
Sand in the blind eye.

MOON-DOG SONG

I stretch my pockets
Wide and find no dimes
Winter has come
I think of the scratch
Of grass of soaking
Berries of monarchs
Winging it on thistles
My head breaks

I search on the side-
Walk my child thinks
I'm looking for dimes
The sun obliquely lights
On her balloon it breaks
I say wait for the time
Of the masks I promise

Her sweets . . . I can't go home
The house has no doors
The windows are heading north
The tapping won't stop
You knock . . . trick or treat
They give you candy
Let's go now she says

But I am shadowed
By a shedding moon-
Dog look I say
Summer's all over
She says . . . let's go home . . .
I take her hand. . . .

BLUE MOON RUMORS

I follow you lost
You love me lonely
I love you welcome
You wave me home
I love you gold
You follow me glowing
I love you pregnant
You hold me dark
I gather you round
You find me pageant
Maiden and Harlot
Diva and Biker
Science and Nasa
Worker and Weaver
Menstrual tidings
Lost tears their shedding
Wax moon retiring
In tides returning
I follow you lost
You find me welcome
You bring me news
I take you home

LOVERS IN THE FREE FALL

When I first came here

I found my future, free falling

Out of a blank

Sky. *No moon . . .*
                                    Oblivion

Covering me

Like a tarp

Till, still slumbering, and somehow lapsed . . .

I slapped down and wised up

Wised up slapped down

To the plausible Earth

Rising up too late for my rescue

Revealing

Our true/ impartial/ partner/ship

Like an open trap

Like a well-used map

Lovers//in the free fall/ lovers/ in the free fall

Lovers Lovers//Lovers in the free fall/ Now

SLAPDOWN/WISE/UP

WHAT YOU WISH FOR

I'm trying to find my metaphor
So I can open up the door
So I can be a butterfly
So I can find my shape

So I can go to market
So toss me a blanket
So I can find my shape

I'm trying to find my metaphor
I'm here without my pinafore
I'm totally exposed

I'm trying to find my metaphor
So I can open up the door
So I can be a butterfly
So I can find my shape

So I can go to market
I'm trying to find my content
So toss me a blanket

I'm trying to find my shape

RESTLESS

The cheetah longs for
The air. Dove longs for the lair
Love longs to be free

Fish longs for the field
The cricket longs for the sea
How 'bout thee and me?

THERE ARE STORIES

I do not want to explain
stories which cause me pain
stories to make fall the rain
stories that speak and have no sound
stories that fall seven stories to the ground
stories that tell and do not tell
stories that are just a little bitty yell
stories that give voice
stories that lift off and rejoice
stories that catabout and carouse
stories that are sweet-skin deep and arouse
stories which suddenly around the next corner
appear and stories which disappear
there are stories born in fire
and stories in the muck n' mire
there are stories my mama knows
and stories my mama will never know
there are stories to curtail
and stories to wail
stories that dawg and stories that zig-
zag stories that are deep rooted and stories to charm
stories to bear arms stories we pray to forget and
stories which are birthdays and beget
stories next time around and not yet and hey it's all
part of one big story ah men and ah women
we hold on and let go one whirl
without end amen

MAX

—for my grandson, Max Jepsen

Max has four protectors
Finny greeny tinny and sunny shiny
And these four have one thousand brothers
And they are all orphans
Some say their real father is god
We don't know much about their mother

Finny is finny
The bravest of the brave
Tinny is the tin man
He always needs oil
Greeny is the green knight
From arthur's round table
He is looking for some glue
To put his head back on
And then there is
Sunny shiny
He has armor which shines
Like the sun

They travel the world together
Having lots of cool adventures
They are always trying
To have fun and
To help people in trouble
And also to fight the bad guys
And to put them into the dungeon
So they will never bother us again

Just recently max's grandmother
Asked max how finny
Got to be so brave

Max said that finny drank

The soup of the universe and mixed it
With the soup of braveness . . .
And he drank the soup quite often
Not just once
And one time he thought he was drinking
The soup of the universe
And guess what he was drinking
The soup of snakes

And he turned into a snake
And his name became snakey
The newest twist in the story goes like this
Everyone in the family of a thousand brothers
Is a twin . . .so finny and finn mc/cool are brothers
And tinny and greeny
And bluey and blacky are twins
And guess what?
They have received some clues
About who their real father is . . .

Sooooooooooo
Stay close and tuned in
For the next chapter
Of max's super adventures

THE LAST OF THE BIG TOPS

My sister and I
We almost died in a circus fire
In Hartford Connecticut
Barnum and Bailey Ringling Brothers
1944
Last of the big tops
I was lucky
So was my sister. So was Mrs. Root
So was Margot Root
We were seated near the open flap
The flames were inside
Outside outside
We had to get outside

I could smell the lions burning
They climbed up on blue pedestals
Or were they green pedestals
Were they seals nosing rubber balls
Or were they trapeze artists
Loop the looping
Was there a clown
Munching lettuce
Or was he holding two pails of water
While the tent was burning

Suddenly this giant rush and rumble
Then people said fire then people pushed then people
Pressed up around us fire fire young men jumping over seats
Trying to get out in front of the rest of us
Mrs root held our hands margot root started to run off for a few seconds in a panic
Mrs root kept holding our hands tightly and yelled, i had never heard mrs root yell
Normally she had a very soft voice this time she was yelling we held on

MARGOT COME BACK
My big sister left her little green turtle with the painted palm tree
She left it on the bench
She wanted to go back inside and get it
But we were on our way to the open flap i see
The look in the eyes of the old couple near me a frightened look big eyes on
Old faces there was a burning smell and when we looked up we could see
Fire creeping along the inside of the tent when we finally got out i could see
Huge orange flames licking up the big top that was my first circus and that
Was the last of the big tops

FISH
—for Etheridge Kmight

When you first arrived
at Indiana State Penitentiary
in Michigan City
that's what you were
fish
you had that fresh/ fish smell
you had that fresh/ fish look
and you had to watch your fresh/ fish back
and when the others came up from Pendleton
no longer juveniles
they were young militant blacks
and you watched
and rejoiced
that's what they were
fish
but a new and dangerous breed
voicing Revolution
by that time
you were in love with fish
you had your own tank
in your cell
and you fell ***in love*** with fish
in the beginning you had the tank for the light
so you could read your way deep
into the night and sink solitary
and reckless into fanon
and malcolm and aj rogers and haki
langston and sonia and gwen and dudley
bly and louis un/te/meyer's an/thol/og/y of modern po/e/try
the title said so slowly and deliberately
you could taste the syllables
and later you fell in love with the fish
you liked to watch them swirl and glide
and sometimes when you were casting out of the pen

and angling for a flip/ tail swish of a thought
you would open up your prison/ vision to the fish
and you knew you were in love
in love with the scent and the ink
in love with the fish
nosing their way up against
the common glass

THEY SAY

They say/ the water has holes in it
And the fish/ fall through
They say/ the glacier/ has osteoporosis
And soon will shrink to nothing
They say the polar bears are groggy refugees
Trudging toward fatality/ they say
Our trees are smoking and we know
That smoking kills
They say the cities are smoldering/ oldering
And after dark the gangs are waiting
For action/ re/action/ and you know who they're after
They say the glove for the right hand
Can never fit the left
They say the left is lost/ and nothing can be done
To retrieve it/ believe it
They say our sun is forever dimmed
And the gases surrounding it are noxious/ noxious
They say there is a blockbuster in our drinking water
And even the fishes of our sea/ are flip/flopping/ belly up/belly up
They say we should not go over ground
Because of the explosions
They say we should not go underground
Because of the bombs
They say only god can save us
And we better not forget it/ forget it
They say we are made in his image/ straight/ up/
No dinos/ chimps /or snakes
Elephants/ or grandmother spiders
No critters/ no critters/ god forbid
Along the rigid spine of our lineage
Can intercede for us
They say we must learn the rules
The drills and applications/ they say we must accept
The irrefutable statistics/ the data /the facts
God preserve us/ and if we don't

We're in big trouble/ big trouble

(They say that falling in love
is wonderful/ wonderful/ so they say)

GERANIUMS
—for my sister, Jenifer Gordon Mumford

It's hard to dream and then reflect
Inside the cranium I sink into the mud
And lore and then by miracle I rise and think
I've caught a fish a little silver fish
At least I thought I caught a silver fish
But maybe I am dreaming love
For Jen who left this world a week ago
She loved the monarch butterfly
She tended red geraniums
Like yours and mine, our craniums, our souls
Our songs, the sinking makes us sing I think
And now the singing makes us strong
I can't be wrong on this I wish
To rest beside a bed of red geraniums
And think about my sister Jen
Taking care of red geraniums
And guarded by a monarch butterfly

VALENTINE

When love rides side saddle
Over the badlands
When love smiles on the ruins
Soaking the sad lands

Will you gamble on love
I ask you again
Will you still welcome love
And begin to begin?

When love calls collect
Will you jump to the call
When love's outta work
Will you give love yr all

Will you gamble on love
Through tears and through time
Will you still welcome love
From an old valentine?

When love surfs the tsunami
When love's on the lam
When love is the loser
Of poetry slams

Will you gamble on love
I ask you again
Will you still welcome love
To the end of the end?

When love seems indifferent
When love bursts yr bubble
When all you can hear
Are the cries from the rubble

Will you gamble on love
Through tears and through time
Will you gamble on love
Till the end of this line?

When love's been laid off
And the checkbook kicks zero
When love's home with the flu
A broken down hero

Will you gamble on love
Through tears and through time
Will you gamble on love
For this old valentine?

When love suffers an earth/quake
When love knows a break/ up
When love gives you heart/break
When love is a shake/ up

Will you gamble on love
I ask you again
Will you gamble on love
To the end of the end

COPS IN THE KITCHEN

There were cops
In the kitchen that day
Bigger than bassoons or tubas
They carried my cousin away
They said they had received complaints
She chanted: and worse:
In a weird wired language
They could not comprehend
The men tramped around the premises
Switching on the lights
Terrifying dust and mice
Before they found her in the kitchen
Chanting up a storm:
Ways to baffle men
Or stall the tide
Or make a stew
And when the cops came in
The mice scampered sideways
The dust billowed
The stew onion-swarmed
Spilled upon the floor
And burned the skidding soles
Of the cursing men
The cops blew whistles
My cousin laughed
And split her sides
The tears ran out
To inundate the kitchen
Of the infidels

BANISHING POEM FOR THE OLD YEAR

Ring round
In wolf town.
In growl.
In bite. In root.
In danger rage
Of mother grown. In
Tear. In father
Found.
In wolf fang.
In bright rip
In father bane. In mother
Bone. In mind. In wild.
In nip. In bite. On grip.
On long wolf howl
On air. On trip.
On ear. On earth. On birth.
On child. On here. On heart.
On hear. On art. On spell.
On well. On heat.
On eat. On heal.
On hope.
On done. On over.
On through.
On done.
On over. On done.
On deal. On chance.
On over. On dance.
On done. On
Over.
On done.
Oh well.
On word.
On truth

PLACES/SPACES

HOW BLUE

The sky stays
Against the snow
Each day
I go out
I come in
I wake up
I move about
I dream
I drive
I go slow
Finding the real
The recoverable
The silver critter
Gliding
Poking
Stealing
Through the body
Of the building
All a-glitter

NOR'EASTER

coltrane on the radio
love supreme
sheets of sound
warm in/side
outside snow coming down
relentless hushpuppy ghosts
while the workers strike
while the soldiers forge and surge
while the movie plays at the circle theatre
while my greatest pleasure is to stay in bed
a long tome
a tomb of time
an inside outside time
a rhyme of home
veering toward
ghosting off
an investigation in the bones
a tree/ mending notion
a tremendous tree/ mending
rooted
in the sift and silt of things
in the unkind tune of kingdoms
in the unwise manner of wise men
in the woman-groan in grown women
out on the road growing toward lands/ end
years end/ beginning my mother's/ spinning
while the blood flows/ the lost blood/ the insomnia
of the old year/ the release/ of the mama
the sloughing off toward peace the best beginning
careening on a roll/ flood out of control/ watch out for the llama
watch out for the pheasant/ watch out for the seemingly/ pleasant/ diver-
sions watch out for the trauma/ snow comin' up again/ and round the corner circu-
lating/ its particular notion/ its genetic/ swirl
while family grows smaller and friends more real
all this continuation in the enduring world

all this crazy rhyme and elation all this desolation and jubilation

got a notion i been rowin' in your ocean
(go slow/ go slow now)
and i/ i been snowin' in your nation all this time
all this crazy rhyme and rune/ all this crazy time and tune
say i/ been knowin'/ in your nation/ all this time
all this crazy
roll of time

NEWTOWN MILL FIRE ASH

1.
Wet cold pre-christmas sunday
We cannot find the ruby red heart of joy
We are advised to keep close to family and we do
We stay in the hearth in the heart
Away from the troubles/ away from the rumble
We are forest animals in outlandish clothes
We are not fierce we do not tremble
We are waiting can you feel us
Inside our hut of straw and wheat
Inside our ice dome/ our yert/ our round house
Inside our cave/ our café/ but never oh never
In the first-grade classroom soundless and still
No chalk smudge on blackboard
No marker on white board
No construction paper no cut outs no coloring
No yellow paper with blue lines
No presents for teacher no fish no hamsters no seedlings
No red christmas flowers no wrappings no silvery rustle of tinsel
No decals no stickers no glue sticks
No books about reptiles
No books about stars
Only something asunder unutterable
Only the shrouds where real cocoons were waiting
To catch caterpillars in spring so butterflies
Can come again it's so quiet here
Where only days ago
The children pushed together letters to make words
And words to make worlds those unknown sentences
And out of that the stories burst unattended
Life-sized bigger than anything the big people had in mind
The children their mouths swollen and overwhelmed
With songs and stories and poems

2.

Carry carry the children
Carry the children along
Out of the deep heart of sorrow
Out further to the deep heart of the world
And in every street back alley country lane
Mountain trail avenue and thoroughfare
Let the people up/ rise and act as a people
Let the people rise up and act as a People

3.

Last night I went to the Walnut St
Coffee Café in Lynn Massachusetts
To be with my family of friends
Millfire Ash playing Christmas songs
Sparkling lights and candy cane posts and
Red fleece stockings by the door
Tiny lights creeping up the dart board
And trailing over the stacked books and way up
High to the board game called LIFE

We are here
All at our tables/ our stations/
Players and people all one
All in our chosen places
And held by our love of the work
And our love of each other
And outside snow

Jon Waterman and Nick Zaino and Adam Zampino
And singer Michelle Zampino
And Dickey Kraus on the harp
And all night like rain the Christmas
Ache and Chanukah chant
The outpouring of chestnuts roasting as usual by the usual fires

What can we do what can we say
All at our tables close/ breathing out/ letting in
In the ways that we do
When we need each other
To hold/ tight and/ lightly/ light and tightly

We sing our stunned heads off
We speak our broken hearts
Till nothing is left
But the scent and residue
Of Newtown Mill Fire Ash

WHEN WE LOVE

We love strongly
We come as guests
And we don't know when to leave
We never learned that, we
Never got instruction on that matter
And now, we are strangely alone
And strangers to ourselves
And our selves are a whole fleet
Of small crafts, setting sail
To a faraway country
We can only smell
We can only name
Through our blind lids
We can only hear at night
When there is a single bell ringing
We can only taste in a tiny berry
Held by a small child, or a person
At the first and final moment
Of hello and goodbye

LAMENT

—Tenants Harbor, Maine

She was daring the waves
Down low ledge at Roaring Spout
Big one took her out.

Her two brothers went
In after her. Reached her twice.
Lost her twice. On three

She went down alone.
Didn't come up. Later on
Her brothers found her.

Night rain leaves its sound.
Storm dies. Surrenders the heart.
Nor'easter departs.

ICARUS

I wanted to soar
Not create a peremptory end to the chase
Or return as if from war changed into a lulled
Babe shelved in a bunting softened
All ready for the inevitable shell/ shocked spill
A tumble I do not remember

Or I can not remember
(It was a lurch of sorts)
Plummeting downward out from that steep hill
As if the wind itself was giving me chase
And my eventual fall could not be softened
Into a buffeted and gentle loll

Or was it a temporary lull
A time of windy happiness remembered
Like clouds in a moist and softened
Sky, made tranquil and, for me, not abruptly sore
In the blazing ride of the chase
Down that treacherous and betraying hill

TOP GUN

I always wanted
To be one
I was so proud
Of my sound
The damage I could do
Makin' rounds
Hands up! Don't shoot
My family called me
The inflictor
I wore my name
Like a badge
I called myself
The conductor
I could be
Small/ deadly/ huge/ dreaded
Long lastin' mean/ man
In the early days
I wanted to be/ clean/ man
I was rarely chosen
For the/ cold/ war/ bold war
I wore my name like a badge
Call me top gun/ top gun
When the others called me *cry/ baby*
I said later for you/ *bye bye/ baby*
I wanted respect/ I persisted
When they said I was
A pussy/ a sissy/ I resisted
All in all/ wanted to be respected
Didn't want/ to be/ neglected
Didn't want to play the fool
Wanted to go to the top gun school
Hands up Don't shoot
Wanted to be heard
Wanted to be appreciated
If you didn't think like me

Believe me I retaliated
Call me/ Call me. Call me

Hands up! Don't shoot!

BLACK LIVES MATTER

Hands up/ Don't shoot
Hands up/ Don't shoot

A river of human beings
Moving up the endless avenues

To the house of detention
The house of correction

Black silhouettes at the barred windows
Wave/ Pound/ Work the lights
Drink in the illuminated night
Freedom dance
We see you/ we see you

One step to give us power
Toward the light/ and toward the dark
One step/ One step/ One step
One step to give us power
Up the endless avenue to the house
Of detention/ the house of correction
Toward the light
And toward the dark

HAP N' LONE

I once thought Happy
Ridiculous . . . didn't know
How happy I was

Till Hap rode into
The sunset on a speckled
Pony. I was left with

Lonely. Didn't know
Lone wanted to rent my one
N' only stable.

Then Hap beat it back
Into my life . . . wanted to
Occupy my home.

NO VACANCY sign
Hung over my bar table
Now I'm all alone.

And that's the sad
And pitiful story
Of Hap. And Lone.

Motion/Commotion

MOST WANTED LIST
—for David Gowdy

Want to circum/navigate the rainbow
Want to let that hummingbird back in
Want to chase the autumn leaves still further
Down Market St. in Central Square in Lynn.

Want to dream with you upon the purple sofa
And hold you till the cows come ringing home
Want to watch the gulls fly forth forever
In front of tiers of windows where we roam.

Want to repeat an old beloved saying
Want to redefine a ragged verse
Want to rejuvenate a stinging story
Want to reinvent a singing curse.

City of night/ City of Sin
You never go out/ the way you went in
City of light/ City begin
You never go out /the way you go in.

TAKE THE TRANS

I want to move across
I want to cross over
I want to take the trans
I want to take a chance
On the trans
But I'm confused
Don't know what to choose
Do I need a transfer
Do I have a Charlie Card
Do I keep on travellin'
I am just unravellin'
Till the end of the line
Till the end of time
I'm confused
Don't know what to choose
If you were me
If I was you
What would you do
What would I do
Till the end of the line
Please advise
Please advise

Trans/figuration
Trans/migration
Trans/discipline
Trans/port
Trans/atlantic
Trans/parent
Trans/formation
Trans/substantiation
Trans/sylvania
Trans/pacific
Transitory trans/story
Trans/gender

Take the trans
I wanna move across
I wanna cross over

JUST ASKING

Even now after
We lost our way home, after
We jumped devil's gulch

For pure thrills, our eyes
Closed, our hands reaching toward
The rush of the dark

Ride, is there something
I have denied, forgotten
To brush across you?

DO THE STEP ASIDE

And let the new dance inside you
Breathe out and take a ride

And let what's there behind you
Take a ride and step aside and . . .
Surprise! You survive! You thrive!

So step back and do the step aside
Then let what's here inside you
Do the step aside and then . . .

We're ready to ride/ to begin
So let the new dance weave and spin
And let the young dancers ride on in

On the crest/ you can rest
On the out wave/ on the in wave
If you want to join in
Be brave and slide in
And do the step aside

O yes come on in and do the step aside
And surprise!
You/ will shine/

That's you
On the ride
Of the rise and fall
Of the wave
That's you
That's you/ and you and you and you that's us/ that's we

Ready to end
Ready to begin
Do the step aside
Do the step aside

79

MOTION/COMMOTION

I like to mosey
You like to mill

You like to rumble
I like to spill

I like to gallivant
You like to gamble

I like to sally forth
You like to ramble

I like to hushaby
You like to drum

You like to signify
I like to hum

I like to gadabout
You like to layabout

I like to glide about
You like to slide about

I like to drift about
You like to stream

You like to roustabout
I like to dream

CALL

You can call me cormorant
And I will call you stranger
You can call me consonant
And I will call you danger
You can call me accident
And I will call you scar
You can call me galaxy
And I will call you star
We can hold each other
Like water and rock
Like the sidewalk and the moon
Like my smoke in your fire
Like all of this and nothing
In the close animal dark
Everything we do and do not do
Will be the swells
Rambling over the rocks
In red rock park
At high tide
Or the seagulls veering back and forth
In front of my three tiers of windows
While nomads wander by from the shelter
Yelling obscenities at their mates
While the ambulances and fire truck sirens
Offer the jazz of the cities
This tiny drop of time drop-
Ping into the pool
Ping surrounded by surrounding circles
If it were possible
We would push away
The heavy years and the heavy objects
We would meet each other
Where the seagulls veer back and forth
Solely soul of the soil
We would toil/ in the name/ of the lively noun

In the name of the/ active/ verb
In the name of the namaste
In the numinous name
In the luminous name
In the numinous luminous name of love

HEY DANGER

Come on in
We're waitin' for this dance to begin
Stand close to cuttin' edge
Next to safety's side
I'll whisper in yr inner ear
Babe it's been a seesaw slide
Ridin' together with you all of these years
Through weather and trauma
And tusslin' and tears
Babe it's been a pre/carious balancin' act
Movin' long side you, and that's a plain fact
So come on in darlin'
And rev up my engine
Some call it poetry
Some call it legend

Come in the front door
And eat at my table
Come in the back door
Settle down in my stable
Play all of your card tricks
And do not deceive me
I'll give you a call back
Show you how to receive me
Call up yr posse
Bring yr sécurité
Free fall outta those shadows
Out of obscurité

The show down is soon
The hour is late
The music is blue
The rhythm is fate
The lights are turned down
All over this city

Don't show me remorse
Regret or self-pity
I know who you are
And I know what you do
So come on in darlin'
I'm waitin' for you

PENELOPE'S TALKIN' BLUES

I first saw you Odyss
Comin' out of the boxcar's side
Holding onto Adam's rib
It can not be denied
I testify

You know that ol' Adam's rib I'm talking 'bout Odyss
The one with the sweet female juice deep down
In the deep/ down/ deep down/ inside
So you'd never no more in these sorrowful days
Say you'd never no more be denied
But you Odyss you tossed that Adam's rib aside
Yeah you tossed it aside
Like a nasty ol' dog bone
Said you couldn't use it on yr ride
Yeah you said you could not use it
On yr personal ride
I testify

You think I don't remember that day
When you looked at me yr wine-dark bride
And said Babe Babe Babe
Babe I gotta ride
You think I don't remember that day
You think you can play me/ play me
Play me for a fool
Well I can tell you Odyss
You learned more about love from me
Than you ever learned in any mothalovin' travellin' school

You think I don't remember that day
When you looked at me
Yr sweet bright lucky Penny
Yr wine dark bride and said
Babe I gotta ride

Gotta avenge my daddy's name
And get me some freedom and some fame
Daddy Daddy Daddy
That's the only name you cried
You looked at me and said babe
Babe Babe Babe I gotta ride
And that's exactly what you did Odyss
That's exactly what you did
(I testify)

And don't think I didn't hear
'Bout all them exploits and adventures
Don't think I didn't hear
'Bout that hussy Circe
When I heard about her I cried for mercy
And don't think I didn't hear about that Cyclops
When I heard about him my belly went flip-flop

And Odyss our home yeah our happy home
Now it's a honky tonk a jukey joint a funky ol' saloon
With all those raggedy/ ass suitors
Crawlin up and down our stairs
And me in my sorrow . . .
I say in my sorrow and despair
Weavin' and unweavin'/ that weavin' wool
Makin' them young boys believe
That soon's I finish
I'll be free to marry one of them
So they can take yr place
Take all that you hold and have
So at night I unravel
So that weavin' cloth never will be finished

And Odyss
While you were over there in Troy

Raisin' up a ruckus
I was back here in Ithaca
Raisin up our boy . . . Telemachus

And those suitors . . . well don't think
I didn't look around once or twice
(*'Cause some of them young boys*
Were kinda nice)

But keep in mind
I am Penelope
Wife of Odysseus
Not calamity/ calliope/ apostrophe
Eternity infinity or poetry
I say I am
Penelope wife of Odysseus
And I've been waiting for twenty long years
For my man to come home from his personal ride
So he can join me/ his wife Penelope
And remain for the rest of time
Right by my side
I testify!

And sometimes I think to myself
Yessirree I think to myself

No matter where he wanders
No matter where he rides
That man Odyss
Is never satisfied

And he won't be either
Till he hightails it cross-country
On an updraft
And takes his righteous place

Right by my side
I testify!
The name's Penelope
Wife of Odysseus
I testify

PENELOPE'S DREAM

I dreamt last night
First birth. Then fucking. Then death.
Animals. I joined the ranks
Of animals tossing and turning
In the maelstrom while the hurricane
Meted out the pressure from weather
Storm surges abound
And I was right with you

You touched me everywhere
On the earth and in the air
The ear the earth
When eth died in my arms
He kept swaying I mean
He kept on saying
The earth the ear world without end
Amen what goes on beyond us
The breath the breadth of it

I am beginning to see you
However disoriented and misconstrued
Wrongly represented and abused
You odysseus in yr own kinky way
You are a man of god

Do you believe in me the child asked
If you don't . . . I won't be free

I felt you loving my time worn body
With all its flaws and weaknesses and sadness
Its deep deflected sorrows and depressions
Its hearted laughter its seedy joys
I was on my stomach waiting for you
My weight on the hard mattress
I waited I weighted for you

You touched me everywhere
You turned me you startled me
You creamed and stirred me
You sugared me you salted me
You put me on the spit
You carried me to market
You carried me home in yr arms
You cried over me
What was I to do
To do oh do doo wha doo wha

In the open bed of our knowing
In the hard bread of our tasting
Something familiar and small
Something not here at all
It's smell and fragrance
It's sting and savor
And in the end its soft warm comfort
Right then and there
After the fact and before
As the bewildered animals wandered
Looking for their homes now gone
And the birds fleeing and the waters
Over and over rushing in

We had no language we had no words only sounds soft murmurs and songs
Sung on the rhythm and the pulse the heart/beat
The hatching of language not knowing where it would take us
As we joined as we joined the creatures in our soaring in our stumbling
In our falling fast and furious in the neighborhood of our sounds
We touched/ our bodies knowing more than we know
Our whole and hungry bodies
Desirous of garden and kitchen domestic animals and wild beasts
Lurching before and after into the light and the dark
The chaos and the order

Our bodies having wandered out preciously alone
Caught up in the category five hurricane
Spun here
And over the arc
Into the final fragility
Into the eye of the storm

LETTER TO AMERICA WRITTEN DURING
LONG WINTER OF 2015 LYNN MA

Dave looks up from the dining room table
Where he is doing something on the computer
He has that serious look that slow imponderable gaze and says
I'm looking up Flagstaff Arizona
Why don't we go there and get outta this damn snow
Let's go babe let's go tomorrow let's clear outta there
Let's go all the way to Flagstaff Arizona

Moving toward Flagstaff
We're out on the highway we're flying we're hitching
And at night when the blinding lights slow me down
I think about You America looming so big and impenetrable
Like a giant motorized hulk
America . . . I see you at the Walnut St. Café in Lynn
When Rozi from Albania appears
Wrapped in your flag and singing Oh Holy Night
And I see you when Etheridge ambles in
From his corner on 4th and Martindale
And says no black man can ever be a citizen
Can ever be president so what the fuck
And I see you America in my swamp yankee dad
Who believed that anyone (aka any white man)
Can do anything if he works hard enough
No problem and I hear you when Woody
Sings home the deportees and I hear you on Sunday
When the Somali women chant up a fiesta
Next to the Flag Pharmacy on Willow St. in Lynn
Run by the Russians and Florinda from D.R. advises
Us on how to say gracias and get the best deal on prescriptions
And now I am stuck in the Milwaukee airport
And it's snowing it's been snowing all night and there's a second
Hand bookstore here in the airport I'm happy
And now I'm in Allston at a party of sex workers
Shining Dark beauties in stilettos and one Cuban man in wing tip shoes

And they're scooping white powder up from a candy bowl
And I'm slipping away quietly and Maria is crying her mascara
Is smearing and I am waiting right on time
For Ferlinghetti to pick me up at the nearest bus stop
Final destination Rebirth of Wonder will I
Have to stay or go far away freeze or fry
All night it is snowing it keeps on
Forever and I look out my high window
And I see you waving America you bitch
Tired and tattered and raggedy and lovely still waving

REFUGEES

We move with alacrity across
The borders defining us, that contested space between
Your country and mine, refugees congested among
Migrants, and refugees pushing fast forward behind
Multiple war zones and finally diving under
Ground, defying the gravity pull of the situation not over . . .

Did you dare think it was over
On your side or mine, between
Your country or mine, under
The explosives and the blaze, among
Refugees and migrants, sprinting from behind
The barricades in flame, and finally free-falling across

The free fall zone like bloody leaves free falling across
Porous borders. *No fence can keep us out now,* we chant as we over-
Come walls we refuse to hide behind
Never mind the heated breath of the pack expanding the space between
You and me, undermining your country and mine as we move among
Human beings overwhelmed and suffering, not under-

Standing the imperative of our own authority; still, we move under-
Ground and begin to tunnel over-
Land, overwhelmed and suffering, we move as a family among
Your tribe and mine, as we recover the drowned and the dragged under
As we keep our vision focused between
Your country and mine, as we slip out and across

Borders we have not begun to move across
Searching out memory and time, over-
Taking the treacherous path between
Your country and mine, moving deftly among
Outstretched arms and waiting buses with closed doors under
Tear gas and razor wires, we are left behind

And stranded in strange places we fear; behind
Makeshift barricades constructed across
Strangled neighborhoods and bombed out buildings, and over
On the opposite side of the city among
Dark figures in a cluster of smoke, we dance between
Crazy quilt and the new moon standing under-

Hope and desolation crossing relentlessly under
Searchlights carving the space between us, leaving behind
Shredded flyers flapping among torn roadmaps we look over. . . .

LOST LANGUAGES

In the beginning we found ourselves lost;
But maybe it was only the languages
Clinging like burrs to our bodies
We lost or the profound silence
Carrying voices remembered forever in blood-
Memory, under a harvest moon

Let's go back to the harvest moon
We grew strong on once in a time of love
And memory, slip-slapping into our blood-
Stream, measuring the tempo of our true bodies
Carrying our waking and working language
Home to a place where we breathe at last . . .

The sailors say we are lost
Though we know we follow the compass moon
And stars to find the others; our language
Carries our history revealing the blood-
Reminders of cruelty when bodies
Were broken and cast into silence

We pause today in a crush of silence
Where we feel finished and somehow lost
And there are no lies left in our bodies
So we start to weep in the fullness of moon
That rises now in a stammer of blood
Beckoning back a pulse of language

At first it is a thrum of language
Then a huge din of silence
Then an opening rinse of blood
Then a wild ride to a place we lost
With tatters for tickets to a new moon-
Show: time to take back our bodies

Where we swim like seals in our silky bodies
Out beyond the realm of language
Into the turning sea with no moon
Where we warmly welcome our mammal selves
Carrying us into abandon at last . . .
And a blessing breaks free in the blood

WHEN LAST SEEN

Was truth wearing a sombrero a beret/ a porkpie/ a war bonnet/ hijab
Was truth last seen in a flowered forties dress from Sal's was truth seen clanging
A dusty Easter bell when last seen was truth riding through Middlesex farms
Sounding the alarm was truth running from a burning building was truth carrying
A rag doll to Aleppo did you see truth at the crossroads in Charlottesville howling
To redo the last scene in the lost election was truth interrogated at the frontier
Between here and Barcelona was truth on a frozen streetcar to nowhere
Near the laundromat of gray desire was truth ever married
To a special needs woman named Justice?

Did truth break parole and catch a freight to the coast was truth caught
In a trans-American sex trafficking scandal is truth working for the people
Of an alien empire does truth live on the edge of the Black Hills the Bad Lands
The Sangre de Cristo does truth hunker down and hide out
In pre-historic mine fields? *Who declared truth to be fake?*
While watching the news was truth shot by a firing squad looking for Lorca
Looking for Tristan in a rowboat submerged in a stagnant swamp
Was truth found drowning at dawn in a water tower does truth have
An undiagnosed mental illness while walking uphill toward god
Is truth permanently disabled?

Is truth fake/ mama/ sweet mama
Is truth fake like they say?

CLOSING/OPENING

SO BE DONE

So be done
Head. Face
It. You
Have a superior
Belly. You will
Bear hoards
Of children:

You found no arrows
In the rainy forest.
Go home, child.
Go home.

FROM THE SACK

From the sack.
How much I wanted from you.
Important it was to me. How?
Understood. You knew how.
It again. Of course you.
I was called on to hear.
Died, I heard it! Then,
those in pain. Before,
I called out to all
in pain before I died
How much shone in there!
How much earned, how
much was sacrificed, how much
heard about,
which I had, often.
How I loved the sack.
A large sack
near me carrying.

You were walking

near me, carrying
a large sack.
How I loved the sack
which I had often
heard about:
how much was sacrificed,
how much was earned, how much
shone in there. I called out
to all in pain. Before I died
I heard it. Then I was called
to hear it again. Of course
you understood. You knew
how important it was to me,
how much I wanted from you,
from the sack.

IF I ASK

If I ask you to come home
Will you? I can still smell sulphur

And the embers of the heart
Perched helplessly

Here on the first fault
Of glacier and family

Frailties. In this place
where a whole town

Might tumble, let me down
Let me down slowly

So I can see you clearly
I am dusty from the fields

And the fortress. I will go
Anywhere you are going.

END OF SUMMER
—for my granddaughter, Chloe Jepsen

Dear Chloe it's true
There are so many blessings
In the deep green sea

Harbor seal dips down
Disappears and flips over
Somewhere we can't see

We wait for high tide
Roving in and pulling out
Sure as summer's end

Burnished seaweed kelp
Surrounds the tidal pools still
As time's beginnings

Rogue shadows intrude
Steal the high sun of summer
Stalk our melon moon

We are lost in last
Summer days' slow busyness
Then we return home

REDWINGS

Climbs the splintered dawn, sliding
down the lacquer of new surfaces

the wings are of such a fine fragility
they burn the air they travel on
they're born again in noon and afternoon

blood and perseverance stain the sky
where Redwings flies at dusk . . . the hills heave warmth
gentle stones hum lullabies

redwings sweeps through dead-
end hush of three am, and somewhere,
there are the faithful sawings of crickets, the minute

sparks of fireflies, in fact the night is full
with travelers, bearing, borning
redwings on toward home

BLACK KNIGHT
—for Etheridge

Out on the free/way
Singin' strong deep languages
On the long haul home

Yeah you can't miss him
Heaviest dude on the haul road
From here to glitten

Glows like a lantern
Yeah he doin' the fandango
Up from Durango

Above the free/way
Say he doin' the tango
With wings for mittens

Out on the free/way
Bear in blues from the belly
On the long haul home. . . .

PETER WHEATSTRAW;
THE DEVIL'S SON IN LAW

He sings for the bones
Of young Trayvon Martin
Down by the crossroads
He sings for the bones

He stares straight ahead
As he speaks up succinctly
No one owns the dead

He sings for the tears
Of three hundred lost schoolgirls
Down by the crossroads
He sings for their cries

What's in the sack
All that's irretrievable
Lost and can not be found

He stares straight ahead
As he speaks up succinctly
No one owns the dead

STAND STILL

Coming to a stand-
                 still
         a heron
         situated
                        and observant
                        follows
              lost light
    into land's end
                  translates autumn air
                          into silence
                          stands
                                 poised
         while

              wanton and wild

    golden rod suddenly nods
         harbor seals
    disappear and dip

                   gulls
                         veer
                   sails
                        billow

    tossed in the hollow

              heron
    in the shallows
              holds
              onto

              a one legged

         stand-still

CHANGE IN THE AIR

The creatures
Are trying out
Their new-
Found
Gestures
Every
Which way
Like penguins.

Nothing
Perfunctory.
Only these
Succinct
Hard won
Motions.

The architects of new meanings
Excite the frozen air
Exit with unexpected eloquence
Flapping their possibilities

Like Prayer Flags
Like Prayer Flags

Where I am

You are

In this fabulous tableau

Look ahead now. . . .

The creatures are taking

Their bows!

GOD

I dig for my dog
He's buried at the bottom
Of daddy's garden

ACKNOWLEDGEMENTS

A profound thank you to all of us LOVERS in the FREE FALL: The free-dom-seekers, the story tellers, the spoken word artists, the students, the teachers, the children whose poems have nourished me, the movers and dancers circling from the inside out, the inhabitants of the margins moving from the outside in, the singers of poems, the poets of the song, the day-dreamers and the moon-watchers, the painters of poetry, the visual verbal travelers: thanks for the music!

And thanks to my family: Jenifer McKim, Jim Jepsen, Chloe and Max, Nana and to my two sisters Jenifer Gordon Mumford, Mimo Gordon Riley and the generous embrace of our extended family. Deep thanks to M.P. Carver my editor, Gus Zagarella my first shapeshifter, to Lisa Graziano my wonderful Leapfrog Press publisher, and to Marge Piercy and Ira Wood with whom *The Red Thread* first found its path forward into print. Thanks to the beloved community of faculty and students of the European Graduate School, and the Walnut Street Tribe from Lynn, Massachusetts. Also to Evaristo Angurria, muralist, and Beyond Walls, an art organization right here in Lynn. Grateful appreciation.

And to David Gowdy my loving compañero, and to the blazing spirit of Etheridge Knight and my 'womantor' Norma Canner, who helped to bring forth my soundings. Respect and love to all of you . . . from Lynn Massachusetts to the rose colored sand that blows from the Sahara onto the disappearing glacier in Saas Fee, Switzerland. ***One Family!***

The following poems from this collection were previously published:

"Alarm," published in *Branching Out*, Lime Rock Press

"Among," published in *POEISIS*, EGS Press

"Change in the Air," published in *POEISIS*, EGS Press

"End of Summer," published in *Routes*, Lime Rock Press

"Fish," published in *The Red Thread*, Leap Frog Press

"[From the Sack]," published in *Wild Women of Lynn*, Ring of Bone Press

"Geraniums," published in *Routes*, Lime Rock Press

"Having Come to Paris," published in *Wild Women of Lynn*, Ring of Bone Press

"How Blue," published in *Branching Out*, Lime Rock Press

"La Lune et Le Trottoir The Moon and the Side Walk," published in *The 2014 Lunar Calendar*

"Last of the Big Tops," published in *Wild Women of Lynn*, Ring of Bone Press

"Letter," published in *Zig Zag Folios Vol. 1*, YesNo Press

"Lovers in the Freefall," published in *Summer Lines*, Lime Rock Press

"Max," published in *Routes*, Lime Rock Press

"Our Ma," published in *Routes*, Lime Rock Press

"Stand Still," published in *Wild Women of Lynn*, Ring of Bone Press

"Valentine," published in *Branching Out*, Lime Rock Press

"When We Love," published in *Muddy River Review*

THE AUTHOR

Photo by Wes Chester

Elizabeth Gordon McKim is an inter-generational poet and performance artist whose roots are in the oral tradition of song, story and chant. She reads, performs, and teaches in the United States and internationally. Known for five previous books of poetry: *Burning Through*, *Body India*, *Family Salt*, *Boat of the Dream* and *The Red Thread*, she has been published in some of the nation's most engaging magazines and anthologies including *Poetry*, *Poiesis* (Canada), *Ploughshares*, *River Styx*, *Painted Bride Quarterly*, *Blue Sofa Review*, *Drumvoices*, *Epoch* and *Wild Women of Lynn*. She has been a visiting poet in hundreds of schools and colleges, and in 2003 was named the Poet Laureate of the European Graduate School for Expressive Arts in Saas Fee, Switzerland, where she spends her summers as Artist in Residence. She is the co-author with Judith Steinbergh of *Beyond Words: Writing Poems with Children*, which has been in print for more than four decades. McKim was a pioneer faculty member of the Expressive Arts Therapies at Lesley University, as well as adjunct and national faculty for the Department of Creative Arts and Learning where she worked with teachers across the United States weaving multidisciplinary arts into school curriculums. She lives in Lynn, MA, where she is known as the *Jazz Poet of Lynn*, an honor she greatly appreciates.

CPSIA information can be obtained
at www.ICGtesting.com
Printed in the USA
LVHW022359140720
660647LV00003B/3